FROM MEMORY'S WARDROBE

by

Philippa Lawrence

Published in 2009. ISBN No: 978-0-9560658-1-0 £5.
Buff Press, 20 Clovelly Way, Orpington, Kent, BR6 0WD.

British Library Cataloguing-in-Publication Data
A catalogue record for this book is available from
the British Library.

Front cover photo: Philippa Lawrence April 1958
by Elizabeth Lawrence

Back cover photo: Philippa Lawrence June 2008
by Mark Chapman

Design by Philippa Lawrence and Anne Stewart

Buff Press Contact: editor@poetrypf.co.uk Tel: 01689 811394

In loving memory of

John Coulling and Roger Jones

and for
Rosemary Glaisyer
Gillian Hutchinson
Anne and Tony Knowles
and
Diana Lloyd

with love and many thanks
for their help and encouragement

CONTENTS

ACKNOWLEDGEMENTS

I am very grateful to so many people for teaching and inspiring me to write poetry, from my parents and maternal grandmother until I was 4 and my first Headmistress, Winifred M Gibson in Hereford, to Dilys Wood and Myra Schneider of *Second Light Network*; and Rose Flint; leader of the *Kingfisher Group* to-day, including Diana Reader Harris, Margaret Beese, Joan Littlewood, Fleur Adcock, Kit Wright, who inspired the idea of *From Memory's Wardrobe*, Robert Hull, Bill Jones, Simon Armitage, Glyn Maxwell, Fay Marshall, Auberon Waugh, Mario Petrucci, Gemma Okell, John Rety, Ruth O'Callaghan, and so many more, plus Cecily Parsley, Hilaire Belloc, all the poets in *The Dragon Book of Verse* and *How to be Well Versed in Poetry*, and those who wrote nursery rhymes and hymns; and to Anne Stewart, creator of *poetry p f* and publisher of this pamphlet under the Buff Press imprint, for her guidance and assistance, without which *From Memory's Wardrobe* would not have seen the light of day for quite some time!

Thank you all very much.

Philippa Lawrence

INTRODUCTION

The *FROM MEMORY'S WARDROBE* idea grew out of an exercise poet Kit Wright gave us on a 1992 Arvon course with Fleur Adcock at Totleigh Barton, Devon: to write a poem about a garment belonging to someone you knew which brought back memories. As I was in Devon again after many years my mind naturally returned to my early childhood near Teignmouth, and I wrote *The Cashmere Jumper* (first called *From Memory's Wardrobe* which is a line from the poem), incidentally one of my first free verse poems. Kit repeated this exercise on a later course, when I wrote *The Pussy Coat* and *The Esteemed Hat,* and the idea was born though none of the other poems here were written specifically for this subject. Thank you, Kit.

My original plan was to illustrate each poem which held up the proceedings until I abandoned this concept! When assembling the collection I decided the body the clothes adorned, its hair and make-up, and their care (Persil is 100 this year!) should count as part of the wardrobe.

The cover shows myself in April 1958 wearing the pale pink mohair coat described in *Status Symbol.* The white felt hat was from Galeries Lafayette in Regent Street, and the white dots on black cotton skirt and blouse (under the fine botany wool black jumper) were from Neatawear. Out of sight are Dolcis pale icing pink leather court shoes with little Louis heels, and a black suede handbag from The Bath Glove Shop in Bristol. This photo was featured on the *Woman's Hour* web page for 7th April 2005 to illustrate my pale pink lipstick mixed from the white Royal Blanc by Dr N J Payot from Galeries Lafayette, about which they interviewed me, being the oldest item of make-up hoarded by a listener – new to e-mailing I responded as an experiment. Amazingly, I wore this outfit to be interviewed by Joan Littlewood at Theatre Workshop, Stratford East – and got the job.

Philippa Lawrence
Salisbury, September2009

PHILIPPA LAWRENCE

Philippa Lawrence grew up in Devon, Hereford, Dorset and Bristol and was trained in Dress, Set and Costume Design and Stage Management, working in the Theatre and TV. She pioneered restoring historic textiles in stately homes, creating conservation centres at Knole, Sevenoaks (Vita Sackville-West's birthplace), Hatfield House and Castle Howard (the TV and film *Brideshead),* and helped set up the original London University affiliated Textile Conservation Centre at Hampton Court. Philippa lectured with her unique slides here (and still does) and in the USA after being awarded a Churchill Travelling Fellowship. She moved to Salisbury in 1986.

Philippa always wrote poetry in traditional forms but losing her voice and reciting poetry as therapy inspired her to take Arvon Foundation and Southampton University courses, and attend day schools, and the Blue Nose Poets. She has read in London, the South and the West Country.

Founder Chairman of Kick Start Poets, Salisbury; former Poetry Representative for The Society of Women Writers and Journalists, and The Betjeman Society, Philippa selected the poems on behalf of Wiltshire for the 1999 and 2006 Autumn issues of *SOUTH* poetry magazine. In 2003 and 2004 she helped children compose Valentine verses to be hung on red laminated card hearts from a bare tree in a courtyard at the National Trust's house, Stourhead.

In 2006 Philippa was awarded an Arts Council grant to give a paper, entitled *Speak for Yourself you Dumb Blonde,* about losing her voice and how reading and writing poetry helped her recovery, during the *Lapidus* (creative words for health and well-being) 10th Anniversary Conference at the University of Kent that April.

Her poetry has won prizes, and been widely published in anthologies, local and national newspapers and poetry journals, translated into Romanian (see *A Real Princess* and *Valentine's Day*), read on Romanian radio and in London during the **poetry pRO** Romanian UK tour for ***poetry p f***, whose bilingual (Eng/Rom) CD, *And the Story So Far...*, features Philippa.

OUT OF THE MOUTHS OF BABES

'What is mutton dressed as lamb?'
my god-child quizzed her Ma.
'Why d'you ask?' 'Cos that's what
Aunt Jenny says you are!'

FACE VALUE

If you're pretty
no one takes you seriously;
if you're not
no one takes you.

THE MINI SKIRT

There was a young lady from Britain
by whom all the men folk were smitten;
the result, it's a cert
of her mauve mini skirt:
'As you *sew* you shall reap', it is written.

THE CASHMERE JUMPER

My memory nestles up
to a classic sage-green cashmere jumper
from better days, pre-War –
twenty seven and sixpence from Harrods –
matted, neck and wrists stretched,
sleeves baggy and creased
after tight rolling up to hide
the unmendable holes in the elbows
and keep cuffs out of the stew pot.
The silk-fine wool smelt faintly of cooking
and Elizabeth Arden face powder.

Before decay took hold
the jumper clung to my mother's
Margaret Lockwood bosom,
brushed by dark hair I loved
to tangle my fingers in –
a cuddlesome baby's pillow.
Later it sagged loose, felted,
all elasticity washed away;
a grey bloom over the clear colour.

Those comforting cashmere Downs
will always be a gentle presence
in my memory's wardrobe
though the jumper
and my mother's youthful
kitten softness and kindness
are long gone; recollections
of my first four years.

THE ESTEEMED HAT

Herbert Johnson of Bond Street's letter said:
'Dear Sir,
Thank you for your esteemed order…'
so we always called the dark tan felt Trilby
(5 guineas, owing for a long time)
my father's esteemed hat.

When my mother died
twenty years after him
the hat was in her attic
in its original box,
the label directing it to
our old Bristol address;
his name on the band inside
which smelt of his bald head
and flaking skin –
perfect provenance for a museum.

But that would have meant
attaching my name to his
in perpetuity
for researchers to see
and speculate on
so, sacrilege
for a magpie history freak,
I threw it away.
I'm half sorry.

THE PUSSY COAT

I curl foetally inside a remembered nest
of red squirrel fur –
plentiful and familiar then –
pussily lining my father's
double-breasted great coat
of rust coloured Harris tweed
made by Watson, Fagestrom and Hughes
(nicknamed 'Weff and Do')
of Hanover Square in 1932,
years before my birth,
the bill probably paid resentfully
at the last ditch.

Daddy once met the Prince of Wales,
who became Duke of Windsor, there:
the charmer was charmed
by this dinky trend-setter
who still had his hair.
'The impression your clothes give
is so important,' Daddy said
'hotel porters
can tell your tailor at a glance.'

The soft, nose-tickling fur was
worn away to the skin along seams
and the inside pocket edges,
the top one hugging
his precious named bespoke label
to his heart.

Crumbled cigar butts lurked
in the lining's lower pockets
to keep the moths away,
their smell mingling with steam train smoke,
bars, petrol, horses and
his shiny Yul Brynner pate,
to linger comfortingly in the warm fur
that seemed to hold me safe again
for a while, now and then,
in my peripatetic childhood.

He cuddled me inside the coat;
opened his arms to welcome
and enfold me in its furry refuge;
too heavy for me to lift
he spread it on my bed
for me to play princess
at the theatrical digs in Richmond
when my baby sister was arriving
in a nursing home away from the bombs.
Born in the saddle, talented at dissembling,
with his classical profile
and a permanent cavalier's wig,
he could have been a film actor
when the Talkies came.

The pussy coat survived
for the first eleven years of my life,
a remnant of happy toddler years in Devon;
then it disappeared, unexplained,
all shreds of security with it.
Forty years later I learnt
it had been pawned and not redeemed.

SLEEPING BEAUTY

‘This year we’ll do *The Sleeping Beauty*
for our Christmas show, children,’
says our beloved headmistress, Miss Gibson,
Froebel trained like Enid Blyton,
who had written the play
in rhyming couplets:
‘here are your scripts –
your characters are underlined in red.’

She hands them round – oh *no*,
surely the Sleeping Beauty isn’t *me*?
It must be a *mistake*!
Just think what they’ll say at home –
the jeers, and my little sister’ll
tear it up and yell: ‘Snot fair!’
so Mummy won’t let me do it
in case the rumpus annoys Daddy
and he stays out late.

‘We’ll read it through – then,
by next week, you can learn Scene I
so we can plan the moves.
Now Pippa, you speak first –
maybe your mother
has a pre-War frock
she can make into
a princess’s gown?’

‘No, *please*, Miss Gibson,
let Sarah be the Sleeping Beauty.’
‘That’s very sweet of you, Pippa,
but you’re just right.
Don’t be nervous, we’ll all help –
you’ve got a good memory
and Mummy can coach you
with your lines at home.

‘You’ll be eight just after Christmas,
a *big* girl!’
So that was that – wonderful but awful.
We read the play out loud –
what fun it would be
if they needn’t know at home.
In the lav I stuff the script
under my Chilprufe vest
and the hated hand-knitted
Fair Isle jumper
that scratched so much.

At home I take the script out
in the shed and hide it
behind Rosemary rabbit’s hutch
when I muck her out and feed her.
I tell no one.
At the rehearsal I remember most of it,
though I’m on every page –
I can see words in my head
once I’ve read them,
and it’s easy to learn rhymes.

One break time I hear Jenny
behind the coat pegs, saying:
'She's not beautiful, it's her long hair...'
I go back home and beg Mummy to cut
off my precious locks like Jenny's.
It'll be easier to wash so she does
but it curls up shorter – Jenny's is straight.
Miss Gibson says nothing
and I'm still the Sleeping Beauty
though I cry in bed –
it'll take ages to grow again.

Mummy runs in to Miss Gibson in town,
and she says what a pity
I've had my locks cropped just now,
and it all comes out.
Mummy rages in and spanks me:
'What a fool you've made me look!
Where did you think you'd get a frock?'

She ties the tail of my cut off hair
which Daddy, who was furious, kept,
on to a tinsel bow
and Kirby Grips it on.
She makes me the beautifullest frock
from a gauzy pale blue and silver
evening gown Cousin Dot sent
in her clothes parcels from America
but Mummy never wore.
I really *am* a princess.

I do everything right
(I still remember a couplet:
"And now I will climb this turret stair
For I have never been up there!")
and don't make a face
when Charles Gethin-Lewis
kisses me awake.
Everyone has come to watch
and it's great fun –
I really *feel* beautiful again!
My sister behaves,
doesn't make a sound,
and Daddy claps long after the rest.

They all say I look like Shirley Temple
with this hair and pat my curls
the way they used to do
at home in Devon when I was three.
I wish this could go on forever,
happily ever after.

A DRESS OF MY OWN

Until we left Devon in Autumn 1942,
three months before my fourth birthday,
I was a cherished child, smiling trustingly
from under Shirley Temple curls,
dancing and singing to the radiogram,
and dressed in flattering clothes
bought by my mother and grandmother
at Harrods or Daniel Neals,
and Spooners in Plymouth.

That winter I was shoe-horned,
complaining, in to last year's
too small clothes.
Unable to undo the tightly strained
buttons of the front flap of my thick
camel leggings which pressed on my bladder
I had an accident as my mother
made me wait for her to undo them
outside the hall lavatory –
Me! Potty trained by two and proud of it.

My mother beat me and shut me in the cellar,
cold and dark and damp, shamed and
screaming. She must have told the doctor
my sore throat was tonsillitis – I don't
know if he believed her but I was sent to
hospital to have them removed.
I never sang again.

Next year, the War still on, my mother's
2nd cousin in New York started sending parcels
of her clothes and her 6 year old daughter's
which did not fit or suit me –
beautiful dresses from expensive shops,
and odd things like unisex beige
matching 'summer camp' shorts and shirts,
not what English children wore.

1953, Coronation year, but the parcels
still came and my dresses were examined
with scathing amazement at boarding school
(paid for by the kind American cousins)
where we wore our own dresses, not uniform,
in the evenings and summer term.
Then, Magic! A friend asked me to ride
with her behind the golden coach in the camera van
her father's company were to film from.
I rang home joyfully but my mother forbade me
to accept – my father was out! – and I fell apart.

My parents had no consciences but my father
was furious to be deprived of the reflected glory;
so my mother told me, for a combined
Christmas and 15th birthday present,
I could *choose* a dress – *new!* – from M & S.
I found a dark grey/green jersey knit
which clung to my 1950s hour-glass figure,
accentuated by bat-wing 'Dolman' sleeves,
and a swirling ballerina length skirt –
not exactly youthful, but flattering nevertheless…

A REAL PRINCESS

The real princess
could feel a dried pea –
a vegetarian's pulse –
bruising her sensitive skin
through twenty feather beds,
as pebbles on Brighton beach
prod through a towel,
and did not sleep a wink.

I cannot concentrate;
shift in my seat
shrugging my shoulders
longing to strip off
my new pure cotton top,
and cut out the harsh label
scratching the base of my neck –
a hidden synthetic rock
amongst the softly flowing
natural fibres.

A BRISTOL CITY GIRL

Revisiting Bristol I remember
my affront, and perplexed concern
as a teenager when men smirked
and laughed appreciatively
at my saying I lived in Bristol.

My father dubbed me 'Gina Suspensionbrigida' –
I wished Isambard Kingdom Brunel
could have designed a bra for my bristols
as Howard Hughes did for Jane Russell.
She said she never wore it
but the Hollywood experts knew how
to support a big bosom on a slight frame –
as with Marilyn Monroe
who was more my shape.
It should be a matter of engineering.

Fifty years on with a two-hour-glass figure now,
I still search fruitlessly,
from the Queen's corsetière down,
with aching spine, for an efficient bra.
Why are they back fastening –
I have no maid or dresser –
sawn off beneath the bust line
and low cut at the back
even for day wear?
Imagine an architect
trying to support
a balcony like that!

THE PENCIL DRESS

A figure hugging second skin,
clinging to mid-calf,
the pencil dress was revolutionary in 1957
after swirly, flared near ankle-length skirts.
I made the dress from glazed cotton,
scraper board patterned, abstract white scratches
on black at 7/6d a yard
from Taylor's in Queen's Road, Bristol;
completely lined with white rayon taffeta,
cheaper than Japsilk, which served as a toile.

The dress had an Audrey Hepburn neckline –
straight across the collar bone –
a seam under the bust
to meet at the spine,
along which I stitched
white velvet ribbon, an inch wide
with a flat bow in front
and streamers to the knees.

A twenty-four inch Lightening zip
fastened the back –
the new fine, supple nylon kind –
easy to step out of the dress
without messing up my pony tail
but too slim to fit
round the ironing board.

Dolcis Princess three inch stilettos, size 4½,
in white kid, slightly pointed,
cost more than the dress at 4 guineas,
with the latest seamless stockings,
creamy fine 15 denier, size 9,
exclusive to Dior at 12/6d a pair.

Twenty five years later
I put the pencil dress with a costume display
to illustrate my theory that the Victorians
were no tinier than us,
as their petite bodices would seem to show.

Perhaps these survivors were saved
because they belonged to a lost girlhood:
first ball gowns, wedding dresses
from before they ended up
with Queen Victoria's 62 inch waist
from bearing many children;
or were treasured relics of ladies who
died young in childbirth or otherwise.

'You see.' I pointed out the pencil dress
to a group of well brought up
eight to twelve year olds,
'I wore that dress when I was eighteen –
look, that's me in the photograph!'
They gasped in amazement
at their statuesque lecturer
before blushing guiltily, eyes cast down
at shuffling trainers.
Q E D!

STATUS SYMBOL

My American grandmother's rich cousin
gave my mother one of her fur coats –
nutria, velvet soft South American coypu,
exclusive and subtly understated –
one autumn after the War
when our cousins were in England again.
Well cared for and used sparingly
(what social occasions were there?!)
and not essential in this climate,
it lasted until after my mother's death
nearly fifty years later.

Sometimes a cheque from Cousin Anne
enabled the nutria coat to winter in Harrods'
cold store, being cleaned and repaired.
I still have the box it was collected in –
pale grey-green
with London landmarks sketched on it
and the Harrods signature everywhere –
full of old letters.

In the Spring of 1959 I took
the coat to Harrods during a visit
to my grandmother in Bedford Park.
Mild though it was
I wore the beautiful nutria
on the train from Bristol –
and the tube from Turnham Green! –
for fear it would be snatched.

My own pale icing-pink mohair coat –
a fashionable successor
to the hated schoolgirl camel –
from Brights of Bristol three years before
was in their carrier bag
which I swung nonchalantly
as I walked from Knightsbridge station.

The Harrods doormen and floorwalkers
bowed, greeting me enthusiastically,
thinking me a debutante
just emerged from rural isolation
or a budding film starlet
as I progressed to the Fur Department.

The frightening lady in charge
welcomed me effusively,
stroking the silky fur,
helping me reverently out of the coat
and admiring the Bergdorf Goodman
label from New York.
When I retraced my steps,
Cinderella-like in my pale pink mohair,
no one gave me the time of day.

FUR FLYING

My mother wore the nutria coat
given her by our American cousin
after the War, twenty years later
for Christmas in snowy West Berlin
before the Wall came down.
I accompanied her in a fake mink coat –
a model named 'Francesca'
styled by H F Greenfield and sons,
furriers of Brighton –
dark black brown, traditionally cut,
bought in a Brighton nearly new shop.

Warm, cosy and light
but incurably glamorous
I still wear this coat in freezing weather
for town and country or church concerts.
Once, alone as my friend was playing his viola
in a Salisbury Cathedral oratorio,
I found my neighbour
overlapping half my seat
so was deferentially led
to the front pew
near Sir Edward Heath.

One sub-zero day
I wore the coat up to London,
wary of unheated trains.
In Regent Street I thought
how nasty cold weather makes people
as they scowled past me
or snapped at me in shops –
strangers usually smile and are pleasant.
Finally a woman upbraided me
for killing defenceless animals –
the Brighton furrier would be proud!

An older friend whose late husband
was a rich business man
who clothed her appropriately
has some beautiful furs in her attic,
long dead like my Brighton market bargains –
1930s fox and marten
whose comfort and flattery I long for
now I have my bus pass
but dare not wear for fear of violence.

One chilly day, too cold for my friend,
she chanced wearing a mink jacket
to drive to Tesco.
The woman behind her at the check-out
stroked the back appreciatively, saying:
'It's wonderful how realistic
they can make it look!'

LADY DAY

25th March 1960, near midnight
in the cramped sitting room of
Joan's top floor flat in a shabby
Georgian house in Bristol's Clifton.

Sash windows rattle, floor boards creak
under a threadbare Persian style carpet;
as hotly crammed people dance
and talk against Acker Bilk's
Stranger on the Shore
on the record player
in the dim light from candles
flickering in Chianti bottles.

The smell of wax, cigarettes and dust
vies with peanuts and crisps,
and pungent punch mixed
in a blue plastic washing up bowl
with a kitchen ladle to scoop it out.

I'd had to collect the money
for this impromptu party
from the cast and crew
during meal breaks from
rehearsals in the studio
because I was the youngest,
and *a girl*, so they said
people wouldn't refuse me –
and no one did.

No time to change from working clothes:
pleated grey flannel skirt
and Daniel Neal's schoolboy shirt –
no trousers allowed for women
except on location then –
hair in a pony tail,
5 foot five in my studio friendly
noiseless black ballet pumps.

Then there *he* was, towering
nearly a foot above me: that
drop-dead-gorgeous young man
from the studio's period farmyard,
chewing a straw as set dressing.
He'd been sent down from Oxford –
too distracted by moon-struck girls
to pass his exams – and talent-spotted
in the King's Road. Dancing,
my head rested on his frayed
but good blue striped cotton shirt,
unusual then, smelling of starch
and him – male but inoffensive.
I can still see his pale arms
glistening with golden hairs,
green eyes appreciative
under his halo of ash blond curls.

'What's your name?' he had asked.
'Pip, short for Philippa .'
'*Philippa!* Such a *beautiful* name
for a *beautiful* girl,
you shouldn't shorten it!'
he breathed attentively
and, from that night on, I never did.

THE ROOT OF THE MATTER

'You've got *dark* roots!'
my old friend and exact contemporary,
not seen for years,
was examining my clothes and make-up,
ranged in their spare room,
with her usual complimentary interest.
I had just touched up the roots of my hair
so was doubly surprised.

Yet this *was* a compliment!
At sixty two I found I had
an Oldie status symbol
showing my hair was not white-rooted,
coloured to recapture youth,
but darker than the strawberry blonde
of forty years with its own colour
still flourishing underneath.

Heaven knows what this is now –
probably darker than the pale chestnut
I daubed *Light and Bright* on
at twenty two to bring back
the blonde of babyhood,
like the Queen and Princess Royal's,
when people patted my head
murmuring: 'Shirley Temple!'

'Stop moaning!' ash blond Roger
had said and *go blonde!'* so I did, and
it became as much a part of my persona
as for Bardot, Thatcher and Princess Diana,
so builders yelling from scaffolding
changed 'Joan Collins!'
to 'Bridgetty Bar-Dott!'

Now I have a white dusting –
silver among the gold at the temples.
My mother's hair, always dark brown,
was only slightly grey at the forehead
when she died at eighty.

That admiring friend went white
at forty, like a Gainsborough lady,
which I'd love to emulate
but it would have to be done
professionally: time-consuming,
unpleasant and expensive –
I've avoided hairdressers all my life.

At boarding school I tried
a 'Raven Rinse' from Woolworths
which turned my neck, face and hands
navy blue, leaving my hair
still light chestnut.
I'm not dying but bleaching!

Inspired by 'Women Who Dye Their Hair', a poem by Janet Fisher on the vexations of a lifetime of *adding* colour to one's hair ('Images of Women', Arrowhead Press in association with Second Light, 2006).

LIPSTICK

Cultivate your lips
throughout the year:
let them flower
in winter hot-house
or summer fields.

Cyclamen or poppy coloured
every hue
from scarlet to sugar pink:
deadly nightshade,
geranium, sweet pea,
anemone, red campion
or puritan Peace Rose pale.

Poised to perfection
whatever the season
or occasion:
prettify your pout
with glamour
from a chalice
of beauty's potent wine.

MIRROR IMAGE

Once I looked like the Gibson Girls
with hair down to my hour-glass waist
but now time's cellulite unfurls
round an Impressionist impaste.

I don't need contact lenses yet
and see my image clear as day:
a sight to make an angel fret
as pancake fights to keep at bay

the crêping up of middle age;
coarsening pores, and hot flush face –
I've definitely reached the stage
for flattering feathers, fur and lace

with a glamorous hat to hide
hair that now halts at shoulder length:
the girl I used to be has died
and *this* is me – God give me strength.

OUT OF THE BLUE

Varicose veins did not,
like the fine blue veins
on the first Queen Elizabeth's
white-lead encrusted bosom,
denote blue blood.
Presumably before World War II
or beyond, when shorter skirts
and sheer stockings revealed them,
varicose veins,
three dimensional and crooked,
were not visible in public.

We are told that they result
from standing to work
at the kitchen sink or cooker,
in a shop or factory –
though the Queen
does a lot of standing
as did her mother, even at a hundred,
with two inch cork soles
on her high heeled court shoes
which kept her out of wet ground
and made the standing softer
as well as adding to her height.

Our ancestors painted themselves
with woad to frighten foes
and, perhaps, give an impression
of blue blood spilt.
Later ladies with grey hair
had blue rinses to make
the white appear whiter than white
like Reckitt's Blue in the washing.

My Latin teacher
took a big, round, blue rimmed
white enamel bowl of water,
and put a Blue bag in the middle
to seep colour to the water's edge,
and told ten year old me
'that was how the Roman Empire spread' –
and the British, I supposed.

Then Persil, which celebrates
its centenary this year,
started washing whiter
without the visible Blue,
and I wrote in a Scripture essay
that Jesus was transfigured,
his raiment becoming so white
that even Persil
could not have washed it any whiter.

SHOE SHINE

At school it was a punishment
to clean the Prefects' shoes –
cheesy tan leather galleons
not in a style I'd choose.

Give me high heeled, laced-up boots
in peat brown glacé kid
and I'll produce the Kiwi tin
and wrestle off its lid,

stroke dark chocolate polish on,
brush to a mirror's shine
and buff with chamois leather pad,
gloating that they are mine.

Bespoke from Anello and Davide –
twenty pounds in seventy three –
photographed on me by Jane Bown,
perfect for work or spree.

SILVER SHOON

Dream shoes – 'Renata' –
Queenly shoes from Italy
in fake snake silver leather
lined with kid and
dainty but substantial
two and a half inch heels.

Sides open with a strap,
sloping vamp edges
with silver leather and net,
wave-shaped, at £3.99
from the Red Cross shop.

Perfect for the rarely worn,
silver striped, flowing, pleated
aquamarine 'mermaid' dress
bought in Bath 25 years ago,
reduced to £4.99
because of a torn sleeve.

The shoes will last my lifetime
as should the Woly silver polish –
£4.50 for a tiny jar –
which revived them completely
after I'd touched up the scuffed toes
with Christmas silver spray.

COST EFFECTIVE

I am not as silky as I manage to look,
sewn from sow's ears, walking through
Eaton Square in the Spring sunshine.
People look appreciatively from cars
at my statuesque 70 year old figure
clad suitably for old Belgravia,
so I *cost* my outfit.

A long aubergine needlecord skirt,
flaring from below the knee to my ankles –
labelled Principles but £18
in Chain Reaction,
Salisbury's nearly new shop –
which just matches the fine calf-length
wool cardigan from Country Casuals,
maybe £70 when a friend's neighbour
gave it to me years ago,
and I painstakingly unpicked
hundreds of black sequins
from the front and lapels.

My ribbed icing-pink cotton top,
scoop-necked and long-sleeved,
cost £8 for two from Q S
and is the exact colour of the shaded
fine silk scarf wound around
my neck and billowing to my waist –
comparatively expensive
at £20 *new* from Monsoon;

a match for the wide-brimmed cotton hat –
£8.99 from a Salisbury market stall –
now swathed with a gauzy
pink and mauve silk scarf
given me by an old lady friend
twenty years ago and fixed
with a pink 'pearl' hat pin – 50p new.
The necklace of shaded pink
quartz teardrops was a present
from my beloved Florida cousins.

The whole outfit was finished off
with a plain dark brown leather
shoulder bag and gloves, two inch M & S
wedged shoes with bows, Jonelle
pewter tights and – not counting
accessories and underwear –
there you have me: silk purse,
sum total: £51.49!

MUSEUM SHOES

When asked, I reply that
my summer
was not healthy
by freak pontificator's standards
but I did walk.

I enjoyed
nearly a week in June
rushing energetically
round London museums
in one of the few
unwelcome heat waves –
my typical bad luck.

My pale pink,
British Home Stores shoes –
peep-toed, sling-backed,
wedge-heeled –
proved blissfully comfortable
even on their first day out.

Yet they curtsied elegantly
to video-ed instructions
in front of the practice
looking glass
in the Last Deb's exhibition
at Kensington Palace.

LOVING MEMORIES

Around me are many visible tokens
of his love and care:
shelves made and put up
with wooden brackets to my design:
hooks for looking glasses
which reflected his face,
and for saucepans, pictures and photographs.
His Burma Star, pendant from thin red ribbon,
his grandfather's silver pocket watch
which I was hugged against
as it ticked in my ear
through the pocket of the rough
blue herring bone tweed jacket
he enfolded me in.

Now I have that coat in my wardrobe
to hug and lay my face on.
The old fashioned Prussian blue
wool dressing gown,
with cord tie belt and trimming,
a handkerchief still in the pocket,
unwashed, full of beloved D N A,
adorns my Victorian dressmaker's stand
on the landing; his retired B B C staff card,
the photo taken the day before he died,
which I greet and kiss in passing,
hangs on a ball bearing chain
around its neck.

HEARTBREAK

That last Valentine's Day
six years ago
you looked so well
tucking in to
The Haunch of Venison's special
at the table where we sat
for our first lunch together
fourteen years before.

You wore the same
blue herring bone tweed jacket
I loved to clutch your arm through
as I trotted beside you
craning my neck
to your six foot three, still,
despite the stoop of years
and viola playing.

What miraculous foresight
prompted me to ask
the waiter to photograph us,
American tourist style?

This photo, the second last of you
nearly two months
before your death
is a perfect record of
the beginning and the end
of our dear friendship
and a tearful solace.

VALENTINE'S DAY

I wore an icing-pink wool skirt
he never saw
to celebrate his memory
though no lunch out awaited me
and no card arrived.

Once he drew me
a green-hearted card
because I told him I don't like red –
so no red roses.

They've changed the décor
in the restaurant
so there was no point taking a peek
at our table.

Valentine's Day
is happier now than before him
when it held
no treasured memories
to comfort me
against universal hype
and bleak exclusion.

The following year
the pink wool skirt – Laura Ashley
from the nearly new shop for £18 –
had been attacked by moths
and had to be thrown away.

PAST GLORIES

Silken dalliance in the wardrobe lies
and there it's likely to remain
for I have so increased in size
I'll never get it on again.

My pencil dress, a sausage skin
fitting my Monroe hour-glass shape;
frilled Bardot gingham, belted in
to nineteen inches on the tape;

mauve tweed mini, a real bum-freeze;
circular felt, waist same as head –
and the triangular *trapeze*
dress, newsprint strewn with roses, red.

I'd be glad of the cupboard space
but couldn't bring myself to sling
reminders of my youthful grace
out this or any other Spring.

OLD HANDS

My hands are worse this winter,
gnarled and sprinkled with age spots;
the nails are ridged and flaking,
rings trapped by my knuckles' knots.

I cannot pull my tights up
so wear short johns and knee highs;
front buttoned dresses, cardies,
trews and skirts with zipping flies.

That thing for putting socks on
was a useless waste of cash
like the jam jar opener
which gave me a nasty gash.

My hands unfurl painfully
curled up in a fake fur muff:
retired from the keyboard,
these poor claws have had enough.

This won a prize in an Oldie competition, printed in July 2008, for which we were given the first line - it is not, happily, true except about the nails and rings, but I do have all the clothes!

THE LEFT OVER GLOVE

I cry for you, Tina,
when I split the forefinger
of my right hand rubber glove.
My tears merge with Fairy Liquid
in the washing up water.

I used to save
my left hand gloves for you,
and you kept your rights,
always pink, for me –
your idea as we chatted
over the dinner dishes
one Christmas.

I sent you a couple
of yellow left hands,
and a cheerful note –
I didn't *know*, and felt
far from cheerful myself –
two weeks before
you threw yourself
under a train.

Now you are at peace
and out of reach
I must consign
this still whole rubber glove
with life left in it,
to the swing bin.